KERRI MAZZARELLA

Table of Contents

A Pelican Book

Teaching Tips for Caregivers and Teachers:

Research shows that one of the best ways for students to learn a new topic is to read about it.

Before Reading

- Read the title and predict what the book will be about.
- Read the "Words to Know" and discuss the meaning of each word.
- Read the back cover to see what the book is about.

During Reading

- When a student gets to a word that is unknown, ask them to look at the rest of the sentence to find clues to help with the meaning of the unknown word.
- Motivate students with praise and encouragement.

After Reading

- Discuss the main idea of the book.
- Ask students to give one detail that they learned in the book.

SIGHT WORDS

a	my	this
has	on	two
I	ride	use
is	the	with

Words to Know

bike

friends

helmet

pedals

sidewalk

wheels

This is my **bike**.

My bike has two **wheels**.

My bike has two **pedals**.

I use a **helmet**.

I ride my bike on the **sidewalk**.

I ride my bike with **friends**.

Index

Written by: Kerri Mazzarella
Design by: Jen Bowers
Series Development: James Earley

Photos: Shutterstock.com/cover ©2021 Gorloff-KV, cover & interior sports icons ©Geanine87; p.3 & 5 ©2009 s_oleg; p.3 & 14 ©2014 Sergey Novikov; p.3 & 11 ©2022 Lizard; p.3 & 9 ©2015 Mariola Kraczowska; p.3 & 13©2013 Monkey Business Images; p.3 & 7 ©2012 bergamont; p.4 ©2009 Maria Bobrova; p.6 ©2018 ZAO2006; p.8 ©2014 Vitaliy Krasovskiy; p.10 ©2020 Jacob Lund; p.12 ©2020 Creativa Images; p.15 ©2011 Pressmaster

Library of Congress PCN Data
Bike /Kerri Mazzarella
My 1st
ISBN 979-8-8873-5323-4 (hard cover)
ISBN 979-8-8873-5408-8 (paperback)
ISBN 979-8-8873-5493-4 (EPUB)
ISBN 979-8-8873-5578-8 (eBook)
Library of Congress Control Number: 2022948431
Printed in the United States of America.

Seahorse Publishing Company
www.seahorsepub.com

Published in the United States
Seahorse Publishing
PO Box 771325
Coral Springs, FL 33077